The Boxed Garage

Also by Kim Nierman Smith

PARK PARALLEL

C O R N I C E Publishing
P. O. Box 657 Joshua Tree, CA 92252
kimniermansmith.com

ISBN (Paperback): 979-8-9868190-1-3
ISBN (Hardcover): 979-8-9868190-5-1
ISBN (Ebook): 979-8-9868190-3-7
Book design: Nuno Moreira, NMDESIGN

The Boxed Garage

Kim Nierman Smith

CORNICE Publishing

For Mom, Marianne and Harriet

INTRODUCTION

I didn't think I had it in me, but there it was. Living in her oscillating reality was difficult, yet at times it provided sanctuary from my own troubles. The lines often blurred. There was rarely a neutral. Sad and happy leapfrogged through the days. This was her now.

My mom's mental and physical health was in decline. Eventually, she needed my full time assistance. The reflective guilts and repetitive okays will eventually lessen. She's gone now.

Poetry provided an outlet and a sense of stability as our roles reversed. After reading her one of my poems, she smiled broadly and proclaimed, "I did that!". It was true.

Woven into this book are my experiences as daughter, caregiver, and companion.

BACKING IN

Trying to remember
what was behind all this
as the door opened
without pressing a remote

She's waiting

The pause button
without repair
So, are you hungry?
Traffic
I'll unload later

OLD FENCE

I'm hungry
I want love
I was left here
here where
where you
are like
me
Alone
in your soft dirt

FALLING IN LOSS

A pool collected
on the wiper blades
from the night before
and stayed put

Pine sapped downward
like rapids stuck in time

The dog marks his
place
Is mine
until
another shows up

LONG BURROW

There's that hole
in the hill
the groundskeepers fill
but just the front
the inside is empty

Now and then
someone digs in
so begins
what makes the end

EAR THE GROUND

Small umbrellas of silence
asking for an excuse

Soft clover cities

Shelter for the worms
winding time

The shoe crushed on

Roads sang
a violent sonata

of pieces of pieces

Resting
for the rest of this

FROM REMEMBER TO REMEMBER

Milk sat on the face
where chocolate
had melted
into the hair stubble

Thought bubbles
helped move the miles
of winter

Stay awake

TUNNEL LOVE

Dream diving
in a long canal
where vines
are lines
that reel in
the songs
not floating

A net caught the rest

Little dog
we're there

MONEY RUNS

It's feeling six
at three

Shapes on the ceiling
shouldn't be

Cars starting
to move away
from the auto
sprinkler spray

Can't sleep

WINTER SALAD

A course of feelings
toasted
roasted
walking a long trail
trees in the blender
a pulse of nuts
oil slicks
taking a side
Run the dishwasher on normal

VACUUMING IN THE SUN

All specks accountable

Glittery listeners

waiting to scatter
their silver words

Birds like windows

SPARE ROOM

The clock turned off
until
further notice
and there's new noises
next door
that lead to
an empty field

The grasses recorded
how things taste the same
and there's no sound
outside
except the leaves of absence

WELL BEINGS

Walking underwater
on slimy rocks
to get there

Warned of pinchers
and protected by
a white cotton sheet

The other side
has green scenery
and a place
to wake up without goggles

COMFORTER COVER

Half the bread
is gone

Missing your mouth

Eating in bed
and doing laundry
daily

Another load
waits
while the next one
bakes

DON'T TOUCH ME, TOUCH ME

Flew into the bubble
A peccable
plastic cave
with lines
for walking inside

Iridescent drips
run innocent

Pushed up faces
touchy cheeks

Fell asleep with wet hair

SMELL THE VINES THROUGH

The rose
caught up
with the jasmine
in competition
for a little passion

The hiding thorns
hurt most

LEARNED LOAFER

Swayed away
from the heard
and spoken

A softness broke in

Barely there

Whys
on idle

What matters
brushes against
without being known
but cared for

SALTED WATER

We've spun
out of what's comfortable

An unfamiliar latch
onto the edge
of bitter

Hanging in for
the sweet
and falling over falls
to float again
with you

DIFFERENT SOCKETS

Inflamed
brain grains
You look insane
We're not the same

Straw draw

Unscathed
Not scattered

maybe

Fill in with softness
repair the connection

A SHORT WALK ON A LONG LEASH

Patience
Virtual check points
Directional cones
Don't go there
physically
The limitless lobes
exist
For now
dream in grasses

THE WRONG IN A RIGHT MIND

Is the water
from a sealed cloud?

What's happening
with the bee queen?

Was my portable
left behind
on the lawn?

Is a mute scream
loud enough?

THE INSANITY OF SANE

I'm not mad
I am upset

Showing up
Counting down
Walking backwards
Looking around

Watch the air
Blowing
Into a stuck on
Smile

The now
Looks
Old

WORKING WITH THE WAIT

hair grows
half inch
sometimes

depending on
the light
overnight

an elevated gaze
raises violet
in the rays

here's another
distraction

A CONTEST OF YEARNS

Have you seen my eyes?
I left them somewhere again

The ants are identical

Cloned dashes
Perfect sutures

Holding it all together
This summer

No, you come to me

Laying here
Keeping white noise
Close

PLACID DREAMING

Have seen the lawn
Felt the trash

A walk
A gate
A choral hum that
won't break

Another
box to take
out

A few hours ago
was just like
A few hours ago
before

VERGE OF LOST

Seeing the door
A key turns

Last one
Felt lasting

A yellow sun sliced

like a pie
like a time

Pieces
click a life

CROISSANT

Everything

between

    Nothing

TIED TO A MOON

Reeled the driveway
but remembered
I forgot to
pick up the shadow

FRENCH TOAST

A love scene of butter
melting
in the arms
of spice

Brown fluffs
bubble on
a grill of savory
recollections

The dishwasher's full
of sticky situations
to be run
on reason

TO BE NOTICED

An altered think
Hot pink
Not pink
Rosiest roses
posing
Picking up
on a rumble
The bumble eats

THE SOOT ON THE SILL

It finally got
to be too
To be tolerable
and ignored
because there
were
Were there things
to do
less gray?

Lemons like to laugh

BRAIN SPOTTING

there's a less than
where that left
those and
these are not
anymore

ever afterward

FLY AWAY DAYS

gravity
gravitas
gravel
grovel
gavel
hollow
halo
heigh
ho
hey no

COLD PARK WARM SHIT

Frozen sweat
Fog
Fallen pine
Found peanut
Soaked feet
Fountain
Free bags
Fried chicken
Fur

HOUNDSTOOTH

A square set free
Let me out
to play
on the edges
of time's arrow
If the leash is long enough

         it's not really there

DON'T PEE ON MY FLOWER

There
Don't there
Yes there

Weep
Don't weep
Yes weep

Stay
Don't stay
Yes stay

Hello

RIGHT TO ROAM

Some do's
where those don't

Do's
do that don't
do that

Like wanting
that want
to do
all over
again

YOU NEED GREEN SHOES TO

Live on an island
and sleep with the trees

Be stuck in a wallet
at a traffic light

Charge the phone
overnight

Know unknown bottoms
are near

Get away with

A TOUGH MOTHER

Her blossom
missed the bloom

Skip that hurt
and pull the scab

I'm hot, I'm cold
I'm told

Don't need a comforter
a sheet will work

I'm covered

STUCK ON THIS STAIR

My music box muscle
aches these days
Away the way
for fumbling frays
    Variable joy
        Vibrating guts
of a scared soul
Looking for a tonic
take away

Way the way

COMBUSTIBLE NUMBS

Feeling the press
of the capable hours
that lead up to
the inescapable play

The day was laid
in front of my face
and I blew the bubble

ASSORTED SORTS

A red eye wakes up
A cat hugs a matching shirt
A nest is made from a stuffed toy
A bud pops overnight

Some don't remember dinner

A wash wasn't dried
A tree holds a sweet smell
A disturbed dust moves away
A light hangs on all day

I think I'll stay

TEARS IN A NET

Flowing
enough
to fill the pond
enough

Day says
just kidding
Night
is the real sway

Settle
Slow
Sink in

GOOD EYES

Two seekers of focus
show up
for the morning rituals

Years pass

Let's share
the same shape
again

COME OUT TO THE GARDEN

Fill up the chair
Unwind your toes
A robe lays on the arm

Rest

Winding rose
A twist of hose
Noses tilt the sky
Jasmine closes the show

WHERE IS HOME

Already broken in enough
to not
create a blister

Breathing just happens
there

When thinking stops
that's it
When lips touch naturally
that's it

The distance is
magnetic

JOY TALK SMALL

Bits and matter

matter

Too many

matters matter too much

Loose parts

return to

bits

A long little bit

ago

matters

OUTED MIND

The chocolate chips
sat on the edge

They could easily
melt now
melt how

Chip away
Is different by the day

Maybe it's not right
Maybe its just different
by the day

A YAWN FOR YESTERDAY

The couch closed in
and a pillow looked desperate
for company

Convincing
Casual
Cornered

Gave in to the comfort
of a calling cushion

WHAT THE HELL

It's a complex of variations
that make a face
Take a second look
grasp a third
and still
I don't understand
why the fourth is fine
except for the changing mouth

IT'S A SCARY SKULL

Eyelashes
are fluttering
the dimmer switches
sticking on
stuck

Rewind the lines
inside
this time bomb body
bind
stopped on a walk sign

YOU SEEING YOU

Split the reflection
so I see okay
in me

A decisive judge
jumps to the background
and tickles my spine
until I don't see wrongs
in me

A laugh doesn't always
say no

CAN I SHOW YOU

Better to ask first
before
making movement towards someone

It will scare them
and
they will never trust again

PARK IN REST

your silk covered eyes
are protected
so you won't feel
the sleep walking workers
making trips
around the times remembered
in reverse
back to
when it all began

WHAT THE BIRDS TALK ABOUT

I'm having mine now
She's having yours later
You're having hers tomorrow
for lunch
And then they sat
in a row and wondered
what was happening
in the tree across the street

MY MOTHER IS AN ANIMAL

An unpredictable
tangle mane
of pen punched notes
and naughty knots
in need of grooming
There's rank
in the realm of make believe
Spliced up seconds
sing a dizzy tune
Speak a tame chord today

PHASES OF THE ROOM

Unnoticed hall walkers
make imprints
as laundry climbs the stairs
Papers get sorted
and empty boxes
look for something to do
Pull the shades
for the dog in his den
Kissed
Miss you soon

WAITING IN A BLUE CHAIR

While curled up
Curls up
Toes curled
Time curls on
This time reverses
that time
The drip drop
tic tocs
turn off time
Time to turn in
to the mourning
of time

DID YOU TAKE A NUMBER

The electronic sign
decided
who was there
The choice was familiar
and comfortable
and happy
The room was full
of unfamiliar faces
standing in line
Why am I here…
The ticket machine
played morning music
as the crowd
waited in confused euphoria

LET ME GO

Slow motion doll
Conductor of dreams
holding her fingers
together with her fingers
together
Sleep away
a way to pass the time
today
to days end
Eyes rest
with tea bags
today
slip away

BONE STRUCTURE

In mine are yours
Time recognizes us apart
because of births
Can I lend you some fat
so our cheeks match
again?
Let's count backward
and blush
again
Beautiful and imperfect
you are once
again

KNOTTY HEART NECKLACE

She has a murmur
Yes
she has a murmur
A promised pinch
A prayer of peace
I'll hold your hand
through this
Can you feel this?

Purple petals opened
then fell like a pulse
as the ceremony concluded
with our breaths

IT'S HARD TO LIVE AND DIE

Babies want out
counting to see blue
in the sky

Life has started unexpectedly
different

Depending on
Dreaming of
Desiring desires

Begins are the best

Middles can't be bothered
with cutting off the ends
counting to see blue
in the sky

Mothers want out

VACANCY

In the mute
corners
of the room
of the mouth
of the couch
Keep the light on
for now
The absence
lessens
when lashes feel
the rain

FREEDOM OF THE FINALS

Doesn't feel quite right
to feel a quite right
Yet, it feels ok
to feel ok

TALKING CLOSET

I hear thinking
in shapes
you can no longer see

In the shade
of a favorite scarf
on a shelf

I hear your shape
thinking
of a favorite shade

THE END OF BEGINNING

I'm not depressed
I mean
I'm extremely depressed
Things have meaning
I meant well
That's the thing

INTENTIONALLY DEFECTIVE

You've seen my moments
and have been them
A head crowns
and it's all over
An imperfect breather
bouncing bucolic
in the backyard
Until pain
heard in the parts
you had no idea
of yet
runs away with
a song
that starts life
over again

FLASH OF UNDERSTANDING

A wound up music box
with a stuck key
can still talk
without a sound

Stillness

a bend in her road
stays silent

Pointer's finger
one last direction
please

Falling tears are silent

EATING THE RIND

Don't leave it behind
Or talk through
your hands
on the way to that
thought

Just as blind
as the exit sign
of an opened envelope

I'm a flown leaf
that once had a tree
and will soon
live in the ground

DAD'S TEETH

Were stored
In a box
In a bank
In a way
that protected us
from thoughts
Mom had the smile
and a thought
in the way
that helped to
protect her

FLOAT SINK FEELING

Ok now what
What
This happy lost space
shows up as circling circles
waiting to stop and stay
for a while
Remembering to find found
when going
is gone

SELLING SAUNTER

A tree feels it's top
as eyelids are falling
and a wave
curls
just like the one before

A nap after lunch
A fan on low
A cup of anything hot

That long drag
up the road
to somewhere
someone told you about

SO, WHAT'S GOING ON

You're the corner of my eye
A sit in the chair
Distant laughs
on a familiar phone call
What else…
I guess
we'll talk tomorrow
Did you
hear from anyone?

The hawk is gone

MULTIDIMENSIONALS

Me moving you
You see
I'm in a shirt
that doesn't flatten

You moving me
Me
I'm living in time slots
and filling up
the spaces so time
can stretch
instead of skip
away time

SWAY

Let's not be still
in this daze
when there is
wild
that the wind spreads

A whistle sings
to the flower's surprise
in a moment
we'll escape from reality
not to be missed

I miss you
most of the time
these days

HALL CABINETS

Those aren't my towels
but I like the color

Used to keep things
forever

This way
down the stairs

Perfume
and makeup

Another story
left here

MEMORY SEEDS

Specks
or spectacles
Crumbs left
to find a walk back
Maybe the wind
will blow hard today

Stirred up

Disorientating the lost
on their way
to disappear another potential

Hurry
Grow big

WINDOW SPOT

A gap in the plot
that needs no filling
A skip of many beats
Who cares
who is smiling
for nothing happening
Sitting in a seat
surrounded by eager ears

Soothing chatter
It doesn't matter

There's a dullness here
I like

THE JOY OF DESK

A square to call home

The pen is good
sitting on the notes
needing a lot
feeling too much

The screen is a pool
in the morning

Calendar
Passwords
Cords

A keyboard is never clean
for long
Longing on this cushion
for a blank reflection

WHOLE SELVES

Like sourdough
needs those stretchy vacancies
Let's not plug our parts
that want hollows

We aren't solid anyway
so
Relieve the pressure
remove your pods
and scream
it's ok

DID YOU CALL ME

A leopard on her back
A cover up
A continuous trip
on barefoot

Smelling
that seventies sachet

I get you

Watch the sash
Eyes rolling

Shake
Stay awake

You're not in the mirror
like the other end
of last week

Or was it the beginning?

TORNADOS OF TRUTH

What a year
for reactions

Catch some breaths

Take temporary shelter
and find the words
that were
before the mind
could figure out
how to lie
to protect itself
from nothing
really

NO WORDS TOO MANY WORDS

Take the gasp
to look at a picture
of your future
four walls

Will it be just like her's
was

A lot to consider

The what's we want
and whys
we want them

You can take the ferry
across
then come back
and stay

QUIET UP

I know it's weird
So, think the thought
The thing you saw
I'm seeing
I know it's weird
Scratch that
Watch this tonight
Throw your air
I know it's weird
Let's dig
to make the point
So, think the thought
I know it's weird

WORKING THROUGH YOUR DUST

There's a sweet spot speed
On an ungraded road
I get
that you don't get it
So
Watch your wheels
drive around the stones
in the middle

Break

The brevity
is brief

FOG AND THE DOGS

I'm the fog

I'm in the dog's
headlights
for now

Will the sun
burn me off
into the fading
sway
of the heart's grays

You're the fog
today

THE FULL IN EMPTY

Warm walls
make a space
for the chair
Here
and over there
Thoughts on loan
to the receptive knots
A lot to consume
Resume

APPLE PERFUME

The sun was a tease
today
Lost in the lint
of a sweater's shake
somehow feels heavier
than yesterday

It's busy out

There's a place to lag
in this fake daytime light

Imagine the scent
if the blossom
stayed behind

THE FLOWERS KNEW

Oxygen for life
no matter the water
waned

The TV buzzed
in the background
changing the guards
and guardians

Don't worry they're safe
You too

Don't take the vase
just yet

She was the fresh petal
on the dresser

MINDING MINE

Thinking ahead a few steps
before thinking ahead
a few times
a day
Claimed the baggage

TIME TURBINES

Decide the ride
with your person

There
next to you

Wait for the lull

Sneak away
on your dimension

This is what jumping
to feel again
is like

IT'S RESERVED

My rose rubbed cheeks
remember the rush
to push sand around
in the afternoon

The place was rest
We got along
here

The sun knows where
to find you
You're not lost
to me

GOING THERE

Drivers need to rest
on the wrong turn road
Turned
over another shell
with nothing underneath
Maybe
that's the point
of the game

REMAINS TO BE UNSEEN

Pulling in
to the picnic spot
Curves led
Soft swerves
We stayed around
We played
around
and laid her down

To wander
To wonder

What animal do you see?

EXTENDED TEMPORARIES

Every summer
there's the cutoff
Old jeans
looked better now
Pull a string
Brush the fringe
No hem
Another season
will feel it's end

ASKING THE AIR

Summer song
Marathon
Thick and stuck
A night soak
Knocking window
Roof balms

Dog noticed the change
of temperature
and went back to sleep

Was it her time?

OH WELL

These days
These long days
These feelings of days
Days
of picking up
the paces to slow down
again
These feelings

Neutral

These short days
These days
again

WALKING INTO A WEB

The morning
was due
and still enough
not to notice
overnight workings
in the parking lot

Got caught
In it

Remember
the remainders
as remnants
as reminiscent
change

TELLING STORIES

The impulse
to reflect ourselves
just right
losing the narrative

Memories
of our melody

One fried over easy
Or scrambled

A toast
for the mind

Maybe, sunny side?

Crack

INDEX

ACKNOWLEDGMENTS

Thanks to the people and events that inspire my every day.

ABOUT THE AUTHOR

Kim Nierman Smith is the author of poetry books,
Park Parallel and *The Boxed Garage*.
She lives in California with her husband and animals.